Vicki J. Kuyper

EVERYDAY
Faith

Spiritual Refreshment
for Women

BARBOUR
PUBLISHING

Introduction

The Bible says that "without *faith* it is impossible to please God" (Hebrews 11:6 NIV, emphasis added). God places the importance of faith at the very top of the list, and the reason is simple: Faith is the key by which we gain access to Him. How can we love Him when we aren't sure He exists? How can we trust Him when we aren't sure He wants to be part of our lives? By faith we come into God's presence and establish a relationship with Him.

Everyday Faith was designed to open your eyes to faith, to take it from word to concept to experience. It is our prayer that as you move through these pages, you will hear God's voice calling you to place your faith in Him in every aspect of your life.

*Without faith it is impossible to please Him,
for he who comes to God must believe that He is,
and that He is a rewarder of those
who diligently seek Him.*

HEBREWS 11:6 NKJV

Contents

Abilities

Gifts

In his grace, God has given us different gifts for doing certain things well.

ROMANS 12:6 NLT

You are a unique woman. Your blend of experience, talents, and personality are gifts you can share with the world. But when you choose to put your faith in God, you also receive "spiritual" gifts. God gives you these abilities so you can help others see Him more clearly. By using gifts such as teaching, serving, or encouragement, you make faith visible. Ask God to help you understand and use the gifts He's so graciously given to you.

No Comparison Necessary

*We will not compare ourselves with
each other as if one of us were better
and another worse. We have far more
interesting things to do with our lives.
Each of us is an original.*

GALATIANS 5:26 MSG

When God created each of us, He wove
together a wonderful woman unlike any
other. But at times it's tempting to gauge
how well we're doing by using other women
as a measuring stick. Faith offers a different
standard. The Bible encourages us to use
our abilities in ways that honor God. Some
abilities may take center stage, while others
work quietly in the background. Just do what
you can with what you have in ways that make
God smile. No comparison necessary.

Abundance

From God's Perspective

Has not God chosen those who are poor in the eyes of the world to be rich in faith and to inherit the kingdom he promised those who love him?

JAMES 2:5 NIV

Being rich in faith is the secret to leading an abundant life. That's because faith allows us to see life from God's perspective. We begin to appreciate how much we have, instead of focusing on what we think we lack. We understand that what's of eternal worth is more valuable than our net worth. We feel rich, regardless of how much, or how little, we own. True abundance flows from the inside out, from God's hand straight to our hearts.

Exceeded Expectations

*"I have come that they may have life,
and that they may have it more
abundantly."*

JOHN 10:10 NKJV

In Jesus' day, the people of Israel were looking
for the Messiah promised in scripture. They
believed this Savior would restore Israel to
its former power and prosperity. Jesus didn't
meet their expectations. He exceeded them.
Jesus offered them an abundance of riches that
couldn't be stolen or lose value, true treasures
like joy, peace, forgiveness, and eternal life.
Jesus offers these same treasures to you.
All you need to do is place
your faith in Him.

Acceptance

Completely!

*The Spirit makes us sure that God will
accept us because of our faith in Christ.*

GALATIANS 5:5 CEV

God accepts you completely. You don't
need to clean up your language, change your
lifestyle, or step inside of a church. Once you
put your faith in Jesus, things between you and
God are made right. Period. But acceptance
is only the first step in this relationship. As
God's Spirit continues working in your heart,
He gives you the desire and strength you need
to mature into who you were created
to be—an amazing woman whose
character reflects God's.

Loving Acceptance

Accept other believers who are weak in faith, and don't argue with them about what they think is right or wrong.

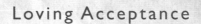

ROMANS 14:1 NLT

Talking about faith can get tricky at times. What you believe, and how faith plays a part in your everyday life, may differ from those around you—even from those who attend the same church. Faith is important. But so is love and acceptance. God wholeheartedly accepts each and every one of His children and asks that we do the same. Listen in love. Learning to accept others the way Jesus did is more important than always seeing eye-to-eye.

Accomplishment

Celebrate!

*We remember before our God
and Father your work produced
by faith, your labor prompted by love,
and your endurance inspired by hope
in our Lord Jesus Christ.*

1 THESSALONIANS 1:3 NIV

When you work hard toward completing a
goal, accomplishing what you've set out to do
is something worth celebrating. When your
accomplishment is fueled by faith, you can
be certain you'll never celebrate alone. God
sees the time, energy, and heart you put into
your work. Better yet, He adds His own power
to your efforts. This means that with God,
you can accomplish things you could never
do solely on your own. That's something truly
worth celebrating—with God!

Appearance

Overflowing with Hope

We live by faith, not by sight.

2 CORINTHIANS 5:7 NIV

Faith changes how we see the world. From all appearances, your circumstances may seem daunting. Your opportunities limited. Your future set in stone. But when you place your faith in God instead of what you see, your heart can't help but overflow with hope. God's power is at work behind the scenes. He's working in both you and your circumstances. He promises to bring something good out of every situation, no matter how things may look on the outside.

Clothe Your Heart

What matters is not your outer appearance—the styling of your hair, the jewelry you wear, the cut of your clothes—but your inner disposition.

1 PETER 3:3-4 MSG

For many women, getting dressed is a bit like painting a portrait. They put themselves together in a way that reflects how they want others to see them. Successful? Confident? Youthful? A bit of a rebel? Who you are within speaks much louder than what you wear without. As you allow God, through faith, to clothe your heart in love and compassion, you'll automatically become more attractive. You'll draw others toward you and God, regardless of what you have on.

Armor of God

Spiritual Arsenal

*Put on all the armor that God gives,
so you can defend yourself against
the devil's tricks.*

EPHESIANS 6:11 CEV

A woman donning armor brings to mind images of Xena the Warrior Princess or Joan of Arc. But the armor God offers is neither fantasy nor outdated. It's a spiritual arsenal of offensive and defensive gear. It's comprised of weapons such as truth, righteousness, peace, and faith. There's a battle going on every day for your mind and heart. But there's no reason to be afraid. Through faith, God's given you everything you need to be victorious.

Courageous Footsteps

*"Blessed is she who has believed
that the Lord would fulfill
his promises to her!"*

LUKE 1:45 NIV

In Jesus' day, women had fewer opportunities to stretch their wings creatively and professionally than they do today. That didn't stop them from holding tightly to God's promises and stepping out to act on what they believed. You can follow in their courageous footsteps. Whatever you believe God wants you to do, big or small, don't hold back. Today, take at least one step toward your goal. With God's help, you'll accomplish everything He's set out for you to do.

Like a Shield

Let your faith be like a shield.

EPHESIANS 6:16 CEV

Some women keep their faith tucked away like a family heirloom, displaying it only on holidays like Easter and Christmas. But if you truly believe what God says is true, faith will be part of your everyday life. Faith is more than words of comfort. It's a shield that can protect you from an assault of doubt or the temptation to do something you know goes against what God's planned for you. Take faith with you wherever you go.

Assurance

He Delivers

*Faith is confidence in what
we hope for and assurance
about what we do not see.*

HEBREWS 11:1 NIV

It's been said that death and taxes are the only
things we can be certain of in our lives. The
Bible tells us that faith brings its own gift of
certainty. Because of God's promises and His
faithfulness in keeping them in the past, we
have the assurance that He'll come through for
us in the future. He's promised we're loved,
forgiven, cared for, and destined for
heaven. Rest in the fact that what God
promises, He delivers.

Secret Ingredient

This is the secret: Christ lives in you.
This gives you assurance
of sharing his glory.

COLOSSIANS 1:27 NLT

When it comes to family recipes, women often remain mum on the secret ingredient that makes their great-grandmother's pot roast, pound cake, or pickled beets stand out from the rest. You have a secret ingredient in your life that assures your future will turn out perfectly. But this secret—that once you put your faith in Jesus, you are assured of spending eternity with Him—is meant for sharing. Pass it on—and you'll be blessing future generations!

Attitude

Drawn Toward Jesus

In your relationships with one another,
have the same mindset as Christ Jesus:
Who, being in very nature God, did not
consider equality with God something to
be used to his own advantage.

PHILIPPIANS 2:5-6 NIV

Even those who don't believe Jesus is God
can agree that He was an extraordinary
person. The way Jesus selflessly loved others,
reaching out to people society cast aside—
including women—demonstrates an attitude
of compassion, humility, and service. We're
drawn to those who sincerely care for us.
That's one reason why we're drawn toward
Jesus. Believing in a God who believes in us
doesn't feel risky. It feels like accepting a free
invitation to be unconditionally loved.

Balance

Let the Spirit renew your thoughts and attitudes. Put on your new nature, created to be like God—truly righteous and holy.

EPHESIANS 4:23-24 NLT

Women are notorious for having moods that shift at the slightest provocation. We may blame it on hormones, stress, or the demands of those around us. Regardless of what pushes our mood swings to an all-time high, the truth is we all need an attitude adjustment now and then. Faith provides exactly what we require. As we turn to God in prayer, His Spirit makes us more like Him. He balances our lives and emotions with His power and perspective.

23

Belief

Faith That Won't Fail

*If Christ wasn't raised to life,
our message is worthless,
and so is your faith.*

1 Corinthians 15:14 cev

Faith, in and of itself, is nothing more than
trust. If you place your trust in something
that isn't trustworthy, your faith is futile. You
can have faith that money grows on trees, but
ultimately that faith isn't going to help you
pay your bills. Putting your faith in Jesus is
different. Historical and biblical eyewitness
accounts back up Jesus' claims. That means
putting your faith in Jesus is both
logical and powerful. It's a faith that
won't fail.

Heart Changes

Jesus went to Galilee preaching the Message of God: "Time's up! God's kingdom is here. Change your life and believe the Message."

MARK 1:14-15 MSG

What you believe will influence the choices you make. If you believe in gravity, you won't jump from a seventh-story balcony to save time in getting to your hair appointment. If you believe what Jesus says, you'll change the way you live. Jesus often talks about the importance of traits such as honesty, purity, and generosity. Though God's Spirit helps change your heart, it's the daily choices you make that bring traits like these to maturity.

Bible

Life Letter

These are written so that you will put your faith in Jesus as the Messiah and the Son of God. If you have faith in him, you will have true life.

JOHN 20:31 CEV

The Bible is like a letter from your best friend. In it, God shares how much He loves you, what He's been up to since the creation of the world, and His plans for the future. You're an important part of those plans. The life you live through faith is the letter you write in return. But others will also sneak a peek at your "life letter." The life you live may be the only Bible some people ever read.

Into Practice

Truth, righteousness, peace, faith, and salvation are more than words. Learn how to apply them. You'll need them throughout your life. God's Word is an indispensable weapon.

EPHESIANS 6:14-17 MSG

What you do with God's words is ultimately what you decide to do with God. If you read the Bible for inspiration, without application, your faith will never be more than a heartwarming pastime. While it's true the Bible can be a source of comfort, it's also a source of power and an instrument of change. Invite God's Spirit to sear the Bible's words into your heart. Then step out in faith and put what you've learned into practice.

Blessings

Believing without Seeing

Jesus said, "So, you believe because you've seen with your own eyes. Even better blessings are in store for those who believe without seeing."

JOHN 20:29 MSG

If you're searching for a pair of shoes, you don't rely on a salesperson's description. You want to see them. Try them on. Walk around in them awhile. The same is true when it comes to trying on faith for size. We long to see the One we've chosen to place our faith in. But Jesus says believing without seeing holds its own special reward. Ask Jesus to help you better understand those blessings as you walk in faith today.

"Nowhere" Blessings

"Turn to face God so he can wipe away your sins, pour out showers of blessing to refresh you, and send you the Messiah he prepared for you, namely, Jesus."

ACTS 3:19-20 MSG

Blessings are gifts straight from God's hand. Some of them are tangible, like the gift of a chance acquaintance leading to a job offer that winds up helping to pay the bills. Some are less concrete. They may come wrapped in things like faith, joy, clarity, and contentment appearing seemingly "out of nowhere" amid difficult circumstances. The more frequently you thank God for His blessings, the more aware you'll be of how many more there are to thank Him for.

Burdens

Personal Trainer

*Give your burdens to the LORD,
and he will take care of you.
He will not permit the godly
to slip and fall.*

PSALM 55:22 NLT

It's important for us women to do some heavy lifting as we age. Weight-bearing exercise helps keep our bones strong and our muscles toned. But bearing mental and emotional weight is another story. These don't build us up. They break us down. Allow faith to become your personal trainer when it comes to what's weighing heavily on your mind and heart. God knows how much weight you can bear. Invite Him to carry what you cannot.

Worries into Prayers

Don't fret or worry. Instead of worrying, pray. Let petitions and praises shape your worries into prayers, letting God know your concerns.

PHILIPPIANS 4:6 MSG

Sometimes it feels like it's a woman's job to worry. If you can't be assured that all of your loved ones' physical and emotional needs are being met, fretting about them makes you feel involved—like you're loving them, even if you're powerless to help. But you know Someone who *does* have the power to help. Anytime you feel the weight of worry, whether it's over someone else's problems or your own, let faith relieve you of the burden. Turn your worries into prayers.

31

Challenge

Head-On

*"If you had faith no larger than
a mustard seed, you could tell this
mountain to move from here to there.
And it would. Everything would
be possible for you."*

MATTHEW 17:20 CEV

The Bible tells us faith is what moves
mountains. Not personal ability. Not
perseverance. Not even prayer. These can all
play a part in facing a challenge that looks as
immovable as a mountain. But it's faith in
God's ability, not our own, that's the first step
toward meeting a challenge head-on—then
conquering it. Remind yourself of what's true
about God's loving character and
incomparable power. Then move
toward the challenge, instead of
away from it. God's in control.

Opportunities

Anyone who meets a testing
challenge head-on and manages to
stick it out is mighty fortunate.
For such persons loyally in love with
God, the reward is life and more life.

JAMES 1:12 MSG

People joke about how women sit around
eating bonbons all day. You know firsthand
nothing is further from the truth. You face
challenges each and every day. Instead of
viewing challenges as negative, faith helps
you see them as opportunities for growth.
In the same way that strengthening your
body is difficult and often uncomfortable,
strengthening your faith can be the same way.
But the outcome is worth the challenge. A
stronger faith results in a more balanced life.

Change

Ultimate Makeover

*Don't become so well-adjusted
to your culture that you fit into it
without even thinking. Instead,
fix your attention on God. You'll be
changed from the inside out.*

ROMANS 12:2 MSG

You're no longer the woman you once were. When you put your faith in God, you experience the ultimate makeover. You're totally forgiven. You're empowered to be able to do whatever God asks. Your old habits lose their grip over you. But continued growth and change is a joint effort between you and God. If there's any area in your life that seems resistant to change, talk to God about it right now—and every morning until change takes place.

"Adieu!"

*"Forget the former things; do not
dwell on the past. See, I am doing
a new thing! Now it springs up;
do you not perceive it?"*

ISAIAH 43:18-19 NIV

Change is a combination of embracing and
letting go. When you become a mom, you
welcome new love and bid "adieu" to some
former freedoms. When you put your faith
in God, you embrace the guidance of God's
Spirit and abandon your old, self-centered
agenda. When times get tough, it's tempting
to seek comfort by looking to the past. But life
only moves in one direction. Forward. Only by
letting go of yesterday can
you welcome today's
opportunities with open
arms.

Character

Testing. . .

*Test yourselves and find out
if you really are true to your faith.
If you pass the test, you will discover
that Christ is living in you.*

2 CORINTHIANS 13:5 CEV

As a kid, you took plenty of tests. Your GPA was determined by how your efforts measured up to a set standard. As a woman of faith, it's time for another test: Measure your character against the woman God desires you to become. This isn't a test God grades. It's simply a tool to help you know where your faith needs to grow. Best of all, this is a group project. Jesus is working both in you and through you.

Pass It On

Each of you is now a new person.
You are becoming more and more
like your Creator, and you will
understand him better.

COLOSSIANS 3:10 CEV

Moms pass on lots of things to their
children, like the shape of their nose or color
of their eyes. They can also pass on things
like speech patterns or lifestyle preferences.
That's because when you spend time together,
you pick up the habits of those you're with.
In the same way, the more time you spend
with God, the more your character begins to
resemble His. That's a family resemblance
worth celebrating.

Children

At Ease

By faith Moses' parents hid him for three months after he was born, because they saw he was no ordinary child, and they were not afraid of the king's edict.

HEBREWS 11:23 NIV

No mother's child is "ordinary." Love enables parents to see their children's unique gifts and potential—and instills in them the desire to protect their children at any cost. Your heavenly Father feels the same way about you and your children. When fear for your children's health or happiness threatens your peace of mind, let faith put your mind at ease. God cares for your children in ways that reach far beyond your own abilities.

Adventurous Tales

It's the living—live men, live women—
who thank you, just as I'm doing right
now. Parents give their children full
reports on your faithful ways.

ISAIAH 38:19 MSG

Tell me a story. . . ." If you're a mom, you've probably heard those words time and time again. But have you ever told your children stories about your faith? How you came to believe in God and how He's been faithful to you in the past are a part of your spiritual family history. The next time a child asks for a story, tell him or her a true tale of wonder and adventure. Tell a tale about God and His love.

Comfort

Limitless

LORD, you know the hopes of the helpless. Surely you will hear their cries and comfort them.

PSALM 10:17 NLT

There's only so much one woman can do. There are limits to your strength, your time, and your capacity to love others well. When you reach the limit of your own abilities, a feeling of helplessness can set in. But being helpless isn't synonymous with being hopeless. God is near. He hears every prayer, every longing, and every sigh. His power, love, and time are limitless. Cry out in faith when you need the comfort of your Father's love.

Changed Hearts

Whatever things were written before were written for our learning, that we through the patience and comfort of the Scriptures might have hope.

ROMANS 15:4 NKJV

Reading how women like us have faced difficult circumstances yet found peace, power, and purpose through faith can be a source of comfort. Whether the account is about Lazarus's sisters Mary and Martha, the woman caught in adultery, or the Samaritan at the well, these women all found comfort in Christ's words. In turn, we can be comforted by their experience. Just as Christ changed their hearts and lives, His words and His love can do the same for us today.

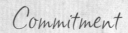

Commitment

Life Preserver

Cling to your faith in Christ.
1 TIMOTHY 1:19 NLT

If you were shipwrecked, you'd cling to your life preserver in hope of rescue. Faith is your life preserver in this world. It keeps your head above water in life and carries you safely into God's arms after death. But it takes commitment to keep holding on tightly. Emotions rise and fall. Circumstances ebb and flow. But God is committed to you. His love and faithfulness never fail. By holding tightly to your faith, you can weather any storm.

Follow Through

By faith the walls of Jericho fell, after the army had marched around them for seven days.

HEBREWS 11:30 NIV

In the Bible, God asks people to do some pretty unlikely things. Build an ark. Defeat Jericho by walking around its walls. Battle a giant with a slingshot. But when people are committed to doing what God asks, amazing things happen. What's God asking you to do? Love someone who seems unlovable? Break a bad habit? Forgive? Commit yourself to follow through and do what God asks. Through faith, you'll witness firsthand how the unbelievable can happen.

Compassion

In Style

*As God's chosen people,
holy and dearly loved, clothe
yourselves with compassion, kindness,
humility, gentleness and patience.*

COLOSSIANS 3:12 NIV

Before you the leave the house, chances
are you make sure you're appropriately
dressed. You don't head out to a business
meeting in your PJs, to the grocery store in
your swimsuit, or off for a jog in heels. Faith
offers you a different kind of wardrobe, one
that's appropriate for every occasion. By
clothing yourself in compassion, you reflect
God's very own style—a style that
always looks good on you and
compliments everyone you meet.

Deeper Than a Mother's Love

"Can a mother forget the baby at her breast and have no compassion on the child she has borne? Though she may forget, I will not forget you!"

ISAIAH **49:15** NIV

A mother's love could be considered the epitome of compassion. A mother selflessly carries a child within her own body for nine months, then nourishes the newborn with her own milk. She comforts, weans, cleans, and cuddles. And if the situation arose, most mothers would sacrifice their own lives to save the children they love. Yet God's compassion runs even deeper than a mother's love. His loving care is passionate, powerful, and permanent for those who put their faith in Him.

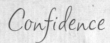

Confidence

God-Confidence

Forget about self-confidence; it's useless.
Cultivate God-confidence.
1 Corinthians 10:12-13 MSG

You're a beautiful, gifted woman. God created you that way. You have countless reasons to be confident in what you do, who you are, and where you're headed—but those reasons don't rest on your talents, intelligence, accomplishments, net worth, or good looks. They rest solely on God and His faithfulness. Living a life of faith means trading self-confidence for God-confidence. It means holding your head high because you know you're loved and that God's Spirit is working through you.

Awed

The Fear-of-God builds up confidence,
and makes a world safe
for your children.

PROVERBS 14:26 MSG

When the Bible talks about the "fear of God," it's more about awe than alarm. Through faith, we catch a glimpse of how powerful God really is and how small we are in comparison. Yet the depth of God's love for us rivals the enormity of His might. Regardless of the troubles that may surround you or what you see on the evening news, you can be confident that God remains in charge, in control, and deeply in love.

47

Contentment

Stuff

*Godliness with contentment
is great gain.*

1 TIMOTHY 6:6 NIV

There's a bumper sticker that claims, "THE ONE WHO DIES WITH THE MOST TOYS WINS." If God wrote a bumper sticker, it might read, "THE ONE WHO'S CONTENT WITH WHAT SHE HAS TRULY LIVES." As your desire for God grows, your longing for more "stuff" takes a distant backseat. That's because through faith you begin to understand how rich you truly are.

God's gifts are better than anything this world has to offer—filling your heart, instead of just your home.

Path to Contentment

"You're blessed when you're content
with just who you are—no more, no less.
That's the moment you find yourselves
proud owners of everything
that can't be bought."

MATTHEW 5:5 MSG

Being content with what you have is one
thing. Being content with who you are is
quite another. This kind of contentment
isn't complacency. It doesn't negate the
importance of striving for excellence or
encouraging growth and change. It means
being at peace with the way God designed
you and the life He's given you. This kind of
contentment is only available in daily doses.
Through faith, seek God and His path to
contentment each and every morning.

Courage

Nothing to Fear

The blood of Jesus gives us courage to enter the most holy place by a new way that leads to life! And this way takes us through the curtain that is Christ himself.

HEBREWS 10:19-20 CEV

Imagine standing before a holy, almighty, and perfect God and being judged for how you've lived your life. Every mistake, poor choice, and moment of rebellion would be exposed. Sounds downright terrifying, doesn't it? But through our faith in Jesus, we have nothing to fear. We stand faultless and forgiven. Through Christ, we can gather the courage to look at ourselves as we really are, faults and all, without shame. Being wholly loved gives us the courage to fully live.

Whatever Needs Done

When I asked for your help,
you answered my prayer
and gave me courage.

PSALM **138:3** CEV

Why do you need courage today? To
apologize? To forgive? To break an old habit?
To discipline a child? To love in the face of
rejection? Courage isn't just for times when
you're facing grievous danger. Any time you
face difficult, unpredictable situations, it
takes courage to move forward. When you're
tempted to turn away from your problems, let
faith help you turn toward God. With Him,
you'll find the courage you
need to do whatever needs
to be done.

Daily Walk

Right Here, Right Now

*Better is one day in your courts
than a thousand elsewhere.*

PSALM 84:10 NIV

It's fun daydreaming about places you'd like
to visit, goals you'd like to accomplish, or the
woman you hope to mature into—someday.
But God's only given you one life. Chances
are, you'll have more dreams than you'll
have days. Instead of living for "someday,"
God challenges you to put your heart into
today. Whether you're sunning on vacation
or scrubbing the kitchen floor, the God of the
universe is right there with you. That's
something worth celebrating!

Into His Arms

"Love the LORD your God,
walk in all his ways, obey his commands,
hold firmly to him, and serve him with
all your heart and all your soul."

JOSHUA 22:5 NLT

Every walk you take is a series of steps that moves you forward. Each day you live is like a single step, moving you closer to—or farther away from—God. That's why it's good to get your bearings each morning. Through reading the Bible and spending time with God in prayer, you'll know which direction to take as you continue your walk of faith. Day by day, God will guide you straight into His arms.

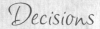

Decisions

Behind the Scenes

We make our own decisions, but the
LORD alone determines what happens.

PROVERBS 16:33 CEV

From the man you choose to marry to how
you style your hair, decisions are part of
your daily life. But that doesn't mean you're
totally in control. Much of life is out of your
hands and solely in God's. That's where
faith provides a place of peace. Rest in the
knowledge that God is working behind the
scenes to bring about good in your life. The
best decision you'll ever make is to trust
in His love for you.

Free Will

*I pray that your love will keep
on growing and that you will fully
know and understand how to
make the right choices.*

PHILIPPIANS 1:9-10 .CEV

Free will is a wonderful gift. It allows you to have a say in the story line of your life. But there are consequences tied to every decision you make, big or small. That's why making wise decisions is so important. The more you allow your faith to influence the decisions you make, the closer you'll be to living the life God desires for you. Invite God into your decision process. Let your "yes" or "no" be preceded by "amen."

55

Desires

Root of Desire

"Wherever your treasure is, there the desires of your heart will also be."

MATTHEW 6:21 NLT

What does your heart long for? If you look at the root of every deep desire, you'll find something only God can fill. Love, security, comfort, significance, joy. . .trying to satisfy these desires apart from God can only yield limited success. God is the only One whose love for you will never waver. You're His treasure and His desire is to spend eternity with you.

As your faith grows, so will your desire to treasure Him in return.

Motivation

*You are no longer ruled by your desires,
but by God's Spirit, who lives in you.*

ROMANS 8:9 CEV

In preparing to play a role, an actress asks
herself, "What's my character's motivation?"
That's because what motivates us, moves us.
If a character's desire is to be admired, rich,
beautiful, or loved, that will influence her
decisions and actions. As you allow God to
work in and through you, your desires begin
to fall in line with His own. There's no longer
any need to act. You're free to be exactly who
God created you to be.

Devotion

Faith on the Move

All the believers devoted themselves to the apostles' teaching, and to fellowship, and to sharing in meals. . .and to prayer.

ACTS 2:42 NLT

The time we set aside to read the Bible and pray each day is often called "daily devotions." Have you ever considered why? Think about what it means to be devoted to your husband, your kids, or your job. Devotion is the commitment of yourself to something or someone you love. The same is true with spiritual devotion. Your spiritual faith is a commitment to love God. And since the word *love* is a verb, an action word, your devotion to God is faith on the move. Where will faith move you today?

Devoted to Others

*Women who claim to be devoted to God
should make themselves attractive by
the good things they do.*

1 TIMOTHY 2:10 NLT

Our devotion to God leads us to be more devoted to others. That's because God's Spirit is at work in us, encouraging us to do what's right. When we keep our promises, weigh our words, and offer a helping hand with no expectation of reward, we are loving God by loving others. Our faith-filled devotion to God brings out the best in us, while at the same time it blesses those around us.

Doubts

Transformed Doubts

Immediately the father of the child
cried out and said with tears,
"Lord, I believe; help my unbelief!"

MARK 9:24 NKJV

Entrusting friends and family to God's
care isn't always easy. One reason is that as
women, we're born caretakers—and we doubt
anyone can care for those we love as well as
we do. Faith assures us that God is the only
perfect Caregiver. When we worry about
someone, we're doubting God's love, power,
and plan for that person's life. Bring every
doubt and worry to God in prayer.

Allow Him to transform your doubts
into faith.

Erased!

When you ask for something, you must have faith and not doubt. Anyone who doubts is like an ocean wave tossed around in a storm.

JAMES 1:6 CEV

You wouldn't ask a gardener to trim your hair or a house painter to paint your nails. When you ask someone to do something, you ask only those who you believe can actually do what needs done. God can do anything that's in line with His will. If you pray without expecting God to answer, doubt is derailing your faith. Ask God to help you understand the "whys" behind your doubts. He can help you erase each one.

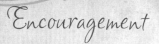

Encouragement

Growing Friendship
and Faith

*When we get together, I want to
encourage you in your faith,
but I also want to be encouraged
by yours.*

ROMANS 1:12 NLT

When women get together, there's usually
a whole lot of talking going on. Conversing,
counseling, giggling, and catching up on the
latest news are all wonderful ways to build a
friendship. But if you want to build your faith,
take time to encourage one another. Tell your
friends how you've seen God at work in their
lives. Share what God's been teaching you.
Ask questions. Pray. Praise. Your friendship
will grow right along with your faith.

You're Loved

*The humble will see their God at work
and be glad. Let all who seek God's
help be encouraged.*

PSALM 69:32 NLT

Asking someone for help can be humbling.
Even if that someone is a close girlfriend.
But if she agrees to assist you and actually
comes through for you, you can't help but
be encouraged. Knowing someone reached
out to you means that person cares. It means
you matter. You're loved. Know that God's
help means the very same thing. He cares *for*
you, because He cares *about* you. Let that fact
encourage you in your faith today.

Eternal Life

Path to Heaven

God loved the people of this world so much that he gave his only Son, so that everyone who has faith in him will have eternal life and never really die.

JOHN 3:16 CEV

Eternal life doesn't begin after you die. It begins the day you put your faith in Jesus' love. Right now, you're in the childhood of eternity. You're learning and growing. Like a toddler trying to master the art of walking, you may wobble a bit at times. But if you fall, God helps get you back on your feet again.

Once your faith sets you on the path toward heaven, nothing—absolutely nothing—can prevent you from reaching your destination.

A Happy Ending

Because you kept on believing,
you'll get what you're looking
forward to: total salvation.

1 PETER 1:9 MSG

Your salvation comes through faith in Christ.
The end result of that salvation is eternal life.
Though you're not home in heaven yet, that
doesn't mean its existence isn't relevant to
you right now. Holding on to your hope of
heaven gives you an eternal perspective. It
frees you from the fear of death, inspires you
to tell others about God's everlasting love, and
reminds you that no matter what you face in
this life, you're guaranteed a happy ending.

Powerful Lessons

Teach believers with your life:
by word, by demeanor, by love,
by faith, by integrity.

1 TIMOTHY 4:12 MSG

As a little girl, perhaps you played "school" before you ever attended class. If you had the coveted role of "teacher," you got to tell your friends what to do. As an adult, you're still playing the role of teacher, whether you're aware of it or not. When what you believe changes the way you live and love, others notice. Who knows? The most powerful lessons you ever teach may be those where you never say a word.

One Worth Following

Follow the example of the correct teaching I gave you, and let the faith and love of Christ Jesus be your model.

2 TIMOTHY 1:13 CEV

The Bible's a pretty thick book. It looks like there's a lot to learn. But Jesus said that if we love God and others, we've fulfilled everything written there. How do we do that? Look to Jesus' own life as recorded in the gospels. Jesus never treats people like an interruption or inconvenience. He listens, comforts, and cares. He spends time with His Father in prayer, regardless of His busy schedule. Jesus' example is one worth following.

Expectations

A Glimpse of God

*In the morning, LORD,
you hear my voice; in the morning
I lay my requests before you
and wait expectantly.*

PSALM 5:3 NIV

If you're expecting an important package, you're often on the lookout for the mail carrier. You peek out the window. Listen for footsteps. Check the mailbox. When you pray, are you on the lookout for God's answers? Not every answer will be delivered when, where, and how you expect. So keep your eyes open and your heart expectant. Don't miss out on the joy of catching a glimpse of God at work.

The Unexpected

Jesus replied, "Why do you say 'if you can'? Anything is possible for someone who has faith!"

MARK 9:23 CEV

What can we expect from God? The unexpected. Many people who came to Jesus asked to be healed. But how Jesus healed them was never the same. He put mud in a blind man's eyes. A bleeding woman merely touched His robe. Sometimes, Jesus spoke— and healing happened. Coming to God in faith means you can expect that He will act. He promises He'll respond to your prayers. How? Anticipate the unexpected.

Faithfulness

An Act of Heart

Let love and faithfulness never leave you;
bind them around your neck, write them on
the tablet of your heart.

PROVERBS 3:3 NIV

Dogs are known as "man's best friend." That's because dogs are faithful. They don't hold a grudge or get so preoccupied with their own lives they forget to greet you at the door. That kind of loyalty comes easy to a dog. But for complex human beings, it takes an act of will—and heart. With God's help, you can become a woman others can depend on. Including God. Live out your faith by becoming more faithful.

Perfectly

*Your kingdom is an everlasting kingdom,
and your dominion endures through all
generations. The LORD is trustworthy in
all he promises and faithful
in all he does.*

PSALM 145:13 NIV

God's faithfulness to you never falters. It began before you were born and will last far beyond the day you die. Nothing you do, or don't do, can adversely affect His love and devotion. This kind of faithfulness can only come from God. Those who love you may promise they'll never let you down, but they're fallible. Just like you. Only God is perfect—and perfectly trustworthy. What He says, He does. Today, tomorrow, always.

Family

Spiritual Leader

A wise woman strengthens her family.

PROVERBS 14:1 NCV

Moms wear many hats. They're called to be chefs, teachers, maids, nurses, mediators, and activity directors—sometimes, all in the same twenty-four-hour period. But God has entrusted you with an even more important role in your family. You're a spiritual leader. As you live out your faith, share the "whys" behind what you do. Point your children in directions that will lead them closer to God.

A strong faith helps build a stronger family.

Learn Today

*Our Lord, in all generations
you have been our home.*

PSALM 90:1 CEV

Your family's unique. You may be married,
single, with kids or without. Parents, siblings,
aunts, cousins. . .they're all part of the family
God's placed you in. That family can be a
testing ground for faith. That's because the
more time you spend with people, the easier it
is for them to rub you the wrong way—and vice
versa. Consider what God wants to teach you
through your family. Patience? Forgiveness?
Grace? Don't put off until tomorrow what you
could learn today.

Feelings

Inside and Out

*God met me more than halfway,
he freed me from my anxious fears.
Look at him; give him your
warmest smile. Never hide
your feelings from him.*

PSALM 34:4-5 MSG

God knows you inside and out. He knows how you feel, right here, right now. So why bother telling Him what's going on in your heart? Because that's how relationships grow. Sharing your personal struggles with a spouse or best friend is a sign of intimacy. It demonstrates your faith in his or her love for you. It also gives the other person an opportunity to offer comfort, help, and hope. God desires that same opportunity in your life.

Control and Clarity

Even if we don't feel at ease,
God is greater than our feelings,
and he knows everything.

1 JOHN 3:20 CEV

Do you regard your emotions as friend or foe? Your answer may depend on how much they control your life. God created you as a woman, an emotional being. Your wide range of emotions—including empathy, anger, compassion, joy, sorrow, and fear—all help you assess situations and decide on appropriate action. But it takes God's wisdom to balance the power of your emotions. When emotions run high, ask God for control and clarity before you act.

Fellowship

Generous

*All the Lord's followers
often met together, and they
shared everything they had.*

ACTS 2:44 CEV

In our culture it's considered admirable to pull yourself up by your own bootstraps—or kitten heel pumps, as the case may be. But God asks His children to walk together, leaning on one another for support. Being generous in sharing our time, our resources, and our experience helps God's family grow stronger as a whole. As we hold on loosely to what we've been given, our arms will be more able to hold on tightly to those around us.

God's Family

*May the God who gives endurance
and encouragement give you the same
attitude of mind toward each other
that Christ Jesus had.*

ROMANS 15:5 NIV

God's family is like your own biological family. You're bound to get along better with some members than with others. When God paints a picture of unity among His people, it doesn't mean disagreements and misunderstandings disappear. It simply means that the faith you share will encourage you to work through any problems that arise. Together as God's family, you can learn what love really looks like, encouraging one another toward growth while helping smooth out each other's rough edges.

Finances

Dollars

*Remember the LORD your God,
for it is he who gives you the
ability to produce wealth.*

DEUTERONOMY 8:18 NIV

A sense of entitlement comes with a paycheck. You earned it, so you get to choose how to spend it, right? But have you ever stopped to consider how the way God created you impacts your ability to earn a living? Take a moment right now to thank God for His part in your financial picture. Ask Him to give you wisdom, self-control, and a spirit of generosity as you choose how to use every dollar you receive.

Just What You Need

*No one can serve two masters. . . . You
cannot serve both God and money.*

MATTHEW 6:24 NIV

When you were a little girl, what was the
"one thing" you wanted? You knew you'd truly
be happy, if only it were yours. Adults often
feel the same way. If only we had more money,
this "one thing" could be ours! But when we
focus on our wants, we become a slave to those
longings. There's only "one thing" that truly
satisfies—having faith in the God who loves
you enough to provide exactly what you need.

Forgiveness

A True Paradise

*If we confess our sins to God,
he can always be trusted to forgive us
and take our sins away.*

1 JOHN 1:9 CEV

Faith and forgiveness are two sides of the same coin. You cannot hold on to one without embracing the other. If you believe that Jesus loves you so much that He would pay the penalty for your sins with His own life, then you must also believe that He wouldn't hold those sins against you any longer. If you're feeling guilty, talk to God. Your feelings are not always truth-tellers. God's forgiveness is what makes spending eternity with Him a true paradise.

Immediately. Completely. Eternally.

Be even-tempered, content with second place, quick to forgive an offense.

COLOSSIANS 3:12-13 MSG

When you put your faith in God, the very first thing He does is forgive you. He doesn't overlook what you've done. He forgives it. Immediately. Completely. Eternally. Choosing to follow His example isn't always easy. But it's always right. When others offend you, don't let your forgiveness hinge on their apology or repentance. You can wisely set boundaries and still offer forgiveness. Ask God to help you forgive before another's fault can fester into a painful, distracting grudge.

Freedom

Free to Be

I will walk in freedom,
for I have devoted
myself to your commandments.

PSALM 119:45 NLT

Without rules, what sounds like freedom can be chaos. Take driving, for instance. You need a license to operate a motor vehicle. That's not because the DMV is worried about your being a woman driver. It's because traffic flows more freely when everyone knows and follows the rules. The same is true when living a life of faith. God's commandments help us build stronger relationships. We're freer to be ourselves and to love God and others well when we follow His rules.

Key to Freedom

The Scriptures declare that we are all prisoners of sin, so we receive God's promise of freedom only by believing in Jesus Christ.

GALATIANS 3:22 NLT

Imagine being locked in prison for years. You're guilty, hopeless, helpless. Then a beloved friend volunteers to take your place. You're set free as another woman takes your punishment as her own. How much do you value the cost of your freedom? In essence, this is what Christ did for you. When you place your faith in Him, you're handed the key to freedom. Honor Jesus' gift by living a life worthy of such sacrifice.

Fresh Start

Anew

The faithful love of the LORD never ends! His mercies never cease. Great is his faithfulness; his mercies begin afresh each morning.

LAMENTATIONS 3:22-23 NLT

We all blow it. We let anger turn our words into weapons. We fall back into patterns we vowed we'd never repeat. We feel ashamed of ourselves as wives, mothers, or friends. But this is another minute, another morning, another chance to begin anew. Faith can break a cycle of regrettable yesterdays—if we let it. God offers forgiveness and a fresh start to all who ask. He never tires of us bringing our brokenness to Him.

An Inside Job

We look inside, and what we see is that anyone united with the Messiah gets a fresh start, is created new. The old life is gone; a new life burgeons!

2 CORINTHIANS 5:17 MSG

Faith is the ultimate makeover. But it doesn't hide who you are with a lift or tuck here and a fresh coat of foundation there. This makeover isn't external. It's eternal. And it's totally an inside job. Jesus referred to it as being "born again." Those old habits, regrets, and mistakes are behind you. Your past is forgiven, and your future empowered by God's Spirit working through you. Let go of yesterday and grab hold of God's promise for today!

Friendship

Make Time

Just as lotions and fragrance give sensual delight, a sweet friendship refreshes the soul.

PROVERBS 27:9 MSG

Jesus' disciples were more than just apprentices learning the ins and outs of faith. They were also Jesus' closest friends. They walked together, talked together, ate together, and prayed together. When Jesus knew His time on earth was short, He turned to them for support. Follow Jesus' example. No matter how busy you get, make time for the friends God brings into your life. They may be God's answers to prayers you're praying today.

Authentic

*Giving an honest answer is
a sign of true friendship.*

PROVERBS 24:26 CEV

Teenage girls are known for being petty and
cliquish. But you're all grown up now. You're
not only a woman, you're a woman of faith.
That means it's time to put away childish
habits, especially those that keep you from
loving others well. A true friend doesn't play
games or hide behind masks. She's honest
about who she is, open about her strengths,
weaknesses, hopes, and fears. Her honesty
invites others to be as authentic with her as
she is with them.

Fruitfulness

Wholesome and Everlasting

"I chose you. I appointed you to go and produce lasting fruit, so that the Father will give you whatever you ask for, using my name."

JOHN 15:16 NLT

Pick up a banana at the supermarket, forget about it for a few days, and *voilà*! You wind up with a black, mushy mess. There's only one kind of fruit that doesn't spoil. That's spiritual fruit. Because of your faith in God, you can trust He's growing wholesome, everlasting fruit in you. You can nurture this fruit, helping it grow to maturity by watering it frequently with God's words. Read the Bible. Then watch what God produces in your life.

Proper Conditions

The Holy Spirit produces this kind of fruit in our lives: love, joy, peace, patience, kindness, goodness, faithfulness, gentleness, and self-control. There is no law against these things!

GALATIANS 5:22-23 NLT

Fruit doesn't ripen through its own hard work. It doesn't will itself to grow juicier. Fruit just does what it was created to do. It grows into something beautiful and beneficial. God's Spirit is the only One who can bring this spiritual fruit to maturity in you. But you can provide the proper conditions to encourage growth. Have faith that God is at work. Put into practice what you learn. Then have patience. Harvest time is coming!

Future

One Step at a Time

Because Jesus was raised from the dead,
we've been given a brand-new
life and have everything to live for,
including a future in heaven—
and the future starts now!

1 PETER 1:3-4 MSG

The future isn't something that's waiting
off in the distance. It's right here, right now.
Every breath you take brings you into that
future, one step at a time. And the future that
awaits you is good. Faith changes the course
of your future as surely as it changes the
landscape of your heart. God is preparing a
home for you that will never be torn down, a
place where your questions will be answered
and your longings, fulfilled.

Worth Waiting For

*"For I know the plans I have for you,"
declares the LORD, "plans to prosper you
and not to harm you, plans to give you
hope and a future."*

JEREMIAH 29:11 NIV

For centuries, people have turned to
fortune-tellers, crystal balls, and horoscopes
in the hope of glimpsing the future. Turning
to anything or anyone other than God for
this kind of information is futile, as well as
forbidden by scripture. It's also unnecessary.
God holds our future in His hands. He has a
plan and a purpose for what lies ahead. We
may not know the details of
all our tomorrows, but faith
assures us it's well worth
waiting for.

Generosity

Bighearted

I am praying that you will put into action the generosity that comes from your faith as you understand and experience all the good things we have in Christ.

PHILEMON 1:6 NLT

When you choose to follow Christ, your faith opens the floodgates of countless good gifts. You receive things like forgiveness, salvation, a future home in heaven, and God's own Spirit living inside you. God's generosity is incomparable. It can also be motivational. When someone is incredibly generous with you, it inspires you to share more generously with others. Whether it's your time, your finances, your home—or things like forgiveness, grace, or love—follow God's example. Be bighearted and openhanded.

Utmost Love and Care

Have you ever come on anything quite like this extravagant generosity of God, this deep, deep wisdom? It's way over our heads. We'll never figure it out.

ROMANS 11:33 MSG

Consider what it would be like to own everything. Absolutely everything. Even the universe is under your control. It seems like it would be easy to be generous. After all, you've got so much. But God treasures every speck of His creation—especially His children. Entrusting us with free will and with the job of caring for this planet was a risky venture. Honor God's generosity by treating His gifts with the utmost love and care.

Of the Heart

Let your gentleness be evident to all.
The Lord is near.

PHILIPPIANS 4:5 NIV

Society honors a gentleman. By definition, he's someone who treats others with courtesy, thoughtfulness, and respect. In contrast, a gentlewoman is often pictured as a proverbial wallflower, soft-spoken, and easily pushed around. Gentleness is a characteristic of the heart—a trait God honors and exemplifies. You can be a spitfire with a voice like a foghorn who's not afraid to stand up for what's right and still exude gentleness. Allow God to help bring out the gentlewoman in you.

Gentle Strength

*Always be prepared to give an answer
to everyone who asks you to give the
reason for the hope that you have.
But do this with gentleness
and respect.*

1 PETER 3:15 NIV

From surgery to tole painting, it takes a
gentle hand to accomplish a delicate task. But
sometimes gentleness is viewed as a sign of
weakness. Gentleness is not less powerful or
effective than strength. It's strength released
in a controlled, appropriate measure. When
sharing your faith, gentleness shows you care
for others the way God does. Jesus was never
pushy. He simply told the truth. Then He
allowed others the freedom
to choose what to do with it.

Goodness

Let Goodness Flow

Whenever we have the opportunity, we should do good to everyone— especially to those in the family of faith.

GALATIANS 6:10 NLT

You can't be a good woman without doing good things. That isn't a rule. It's more of a reminder. Goodness flows naturally from a faith-filled heart. As you grow in your faith, you're changed from the inside out. You become more loving as you draw closer to our loving God. Your once prideful, self-centered heart begins to put others' needs before your own. Say *yes* to letting goodness flow freely from your life into the lives of others.

Good Meals

*He satisfies the longing soul, and fills the
hungry soul with goodness.*

PSALM 107:9 NKJV

When you're preparing a holiday meal, chances
are you don't settle for "good enough." You rely
on your favorite dishes, ones that look good,
taste good, and are good for you. God feeds your
soul similar spiritual fare. Like a good cook who
consistently turns out good meals, our good
God consistently bestows good gifts. Sometimes
they're delectable delights. Other times they're
much needed vegetables. You can trust in God's
goodness to serve up exactly what you need.

Grace

By Grace Alone

God saved you by his grace when you believed. And you can't take credit for this; it is a gift from God.

EPHESIANS 2:8 NLT

It's humbling to accept a favor from someone, especially when you know it's one you can never repay. But that's what grace is: a gift so big you don't deserve it and can never repay it. All God asks is a tiny, mustard seed-sized grain of faith in return. When you tell God, "I believe," His grace wipes away everything that once came between you and Him. Lies. Anger. Betrayal. Pride. Selfishness. They're history, by God's grace alone.

Unfailing Love

Even though on the outside it often looks like things are falling apart on us, on the inside, where God is making new life, not a day goes by without his unfolding grace.

2 CORINTHIANS 4:16 MSG

When you first chose to believe in God, His grace wiped away every past digression you'd ever made from the life He designed for you to lead. But His grace doesn't stop there. Every day, it's at work. You may be God's daughter, but you're still growing. There'll be times you'll stumble. Times you'll look to yourself first, instead of to God. God's grace continues to cleanse you and draw you closer to Him, reassuring you of His unfailing love.

Guidance

Keep Walking

Keep your eyes on Jesus, who both began and finished this race we're in. Study how he did it. Because he never lost sight of where he was headed.

HEBREWS 12:2 MSG

When following a trail, you're really following those who came before you. Physically, they're no longer present. But you can follow what they left behind. Maybe a cairn points you in the proper direction. Perhaps you walk a path flattened by previous footfalls. Keep your eyes on Jesus the way you follow a trail. Read what other followers left behind—the Bible. Watch for signs of God's work in the world. Then keep walking, leaving a "faith trail" others can follow.

The Right Direction

*Each morning let me learn more about
your love because I trust you. I come to
you in prayer, asking for your guidance.*

PSALM 143:8 CEV

If you're navigating a road trip, just owning a map isn't going to get you to your destination. You need to compare where you are on the map with where you want to go, follow road signs, and evaluate your progress. God's Spirit works in much the same way. Each morning ask Him to help you head in the right direction. Then throughout the day, evaluate whether you are where and who you believe God wants you to be.

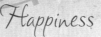
Happiness

Surprised by Happiness

*You will come to know God even better.
His glorious power will make you
patient and strong enough to endure
anything, and you will be truly happy.*

COLOSSIANS 1:10-11 CEV

Faith is a journey. Like any journey, it's a
mixed bag of experiences. You can celebrate
grand vistas then slog through bogs of mud—
all in the same day. Though happiness is
often dependent on circumstances, when
your journey's guided by faith you can find
yourself feeling happy at the most unexpected
moments. Perhaps God brings a Bible verse to
mind that encourages you. Maybe you see Him
at work in a "coincidence." Where will
God surprise you with happiness today?

More to Love

*Make me as happy as you did
when you saved me;
make we want to obey!*

PSALM 51:12 CEV

Relationships grow and change. If you're in a marriage relationship, recall that honeymoon phase. Loving each other seemed easy and exciting, pretty much all the time. Then came everyday life. Apathy crept in. The happiness you first felt seemed to fade. The same thing can happen with God. Don't settle for apathy when there's always more to love and discover about God. (And people!) Ask God to help you look at those you love, including Him, with fresh eyes.

Health

Spiritual Health Care

*The prayer offered in faith
will make the sick person well;
the Lord will raise them up.*

JAMES 5:15 NIV

Prayer is God's spiritual healthcare plan. Modern medicine can do wonderful things to help a sick person get well. But God knows your body better than anyone. He designed it. He can heal it. Not every prayer for healing is answered in the way and time frame we hope for. Sometimes emotional or spiritual healing takes place, while physical healing does not.

God can raise us up in different ways. So call on Him. You never need an appointment.

Safe in His Arms

My health may fail, and my spirit
may grow weak, but God remains the
strength of my heart; he is mine forever.

PSALM 73:26 NLT

Our bodies are miraculous works of art. But they don't last forever. When you're ill or in pain, God is near. As any parent who's ever loved a child knows, He aches with you, as well as for you. When the hope of healing seems distant, if you've run out of words to pray, picture yourself safe in His arms. Wait quietly, expectantly. Listen for His words of comfort. Rest in His promised peace. Hold on to Him for strength.

Help

Anytime, Anywhere

Get up and pray for help all through the night. Pour out your feelings to the Lord, as you would pour water out of a jug.

LAMENTATIONS 2:19 CEV

There's probably no more common prayer than the word *help*. Even those who aren't aware they're calling out to the living God cry out for help in times of despair, fear, or pain. But you know God is near. You know He hears. In faith, you believe He will help. Regardless of your circumstance—big or small—don't wait until you come to the end of your rope to pray. Call out to Him anytime, anywhere.

Invite God

God is our refuge and strength, a very present help in trouble.

PSALM 46:1 NKJV

Real life doesn't resemble what's seen on TV. Problems aren't resolved in an hour's time. There may be seasons where you need God's help just to make it through today and tomorrow and the day after that. During times like these, God's presence can be a place of rest and refuge. Go for a walk. Draw a bubble bath. Find a quiet spot to just sit. Then invite God to join you. Allow Him to refresh you with His love.

Hope

More Reasons to Hope

Let us hold unswervingly to the hope we profess, for he who promised is faithful.

HEBREWS 10:23 NIV

What do you hope for? *Really* hope for? Perhaps it's security, significance, or a relationship that will never let you down. Hopes like these are fulfilled solely through faith. Read God's track record as recorded in the Bible. He keeps His promises in every area time and again. It's true that it takes faith to place your hope in someone you can't see. But you're building your own track record with God. Day by day, you'll discover more reasons to hope in Him.

Hope of Heaven

*What you hope for is kept safe for you
in heaven. You first heard about this
hope when you believed the true
message, which is the good news.*

COLOSSIANS 1:5 CEV

Faith gives us many reasons for hope. A
home in heaven is just one of them. But what
exactly are you hoping for? The Bible tells us
we'll receive a new body, one that never grows
ill or old. Tears will be a thing of the past. We'll
be in the company of angels, other believers,
and God Himself. Scripture tells us words
cannot fully describe what we'll find there.
That's a hope worth holding on to.

Humility

Who Do You See?

Do not think of yourself more highly than you ought, but rather think of yourself with sober judgment, in accordance with the measure of faith God has distributed to each of you.

ROMANS 12:3 NIV

A humble woman sees herself through God's eyes. She recognizes the unique strengths God has built into her character. She sees herself as a creative collage of personality traits, talents, and abilities. But she's also well aware of her weaknesses. She knows that without God, even her strengths would not be enough to catapult her into becoming the woman she wants to be. Look at yourself through God's eyes today. Whom do you see?

The Ultimate Gardener

*In simple humility, let our gardener, God,
landscape you with the Word,
making a salvation-garden of your life.*

JAMES 1:21 MSG

Some women have a bona fide green thumb.
They take a seemingly dead stick and nurture
it into a verdant piece of paradise. Consider
how ridiculous it would be for that once sickly
stick to brag to his foliage friends about the
great turnaround he'd accomplished in his
own life. Obviously, all credit goes to the
gardener. God is the ultimate Gardener. His
focus is tending His children. Humbly allow
Him to have His way in
helping your faith grow.

Integrity

Fully Live

*I will be careful to live a blameless
life. . . . I will lead a life of integrity
in my own home.*

PSALM 101:2 NLT

One of the hardest places to consistently
live out what you believe is in your own
home. That's because those who know you
best have seen you at your worst. Living a
life of integrity 24/7 takes more than self-
control. It takes a change of heart. Only God
can transform a selfish, wayward ego into a
woman worth emulating. Place your faith in
God's power, put your pride on the
line, and then fully live what you say
you believe.

God's Way

In everything set them an example by doing what is good. In your teaching show integrity, seriousness and soundness of speech.

TITUS 2:7-8 NIV

It's said that *character* is who you are in the dark. If integrity is part of that character, you'll do the right thing whether someone's watching or not. It takes faith to remain morally upright, honest, and true to your word in a culture where it's considered acceptable to do the exact opposite in the name of getting ahead. But God's way is ultimately the wisest, most beneficial way. Through your integrity, God may teach others lessons they'll never forget.

Joy

Reserve of Joy

*Though you have not seen him, you love
him; and even though you do not see
him now, you believe in him and are
filled with an inexpressible
and glorious joy.*

1 PETER 1:8 NIV

In the Declaration of Independence,
American citizens are guaranteed the right to
the "pursuit of happiness." That's probably
because happiness is something that must
constantly be pursued. Even if you catch it,
you can't hold on to it. Joy, on the other hand,
is a gift of dependence. The more you depend
on God, the deeper your well of joy. Ask God to
show you how to draw on that reserve of joy in
any and every circumstance.

Unlikely Ways

*When troubles come your way, consider
it an opportunity for great joy. For you
know that when your faith is tested,
your endurance has a chance to grow.*

JAMES 1:2-3 NLT

"Trouble" and "joy" may seem an unlikely
pair, something akin to sardines and
chocolate syrup. But God seems to prefer the
unlikely. He chose a speech-impaired Moses
as His spokesman, and simple fishermen
as missionaries. These choices brought
challenges. But when faith is pushed to its
limits, God works in wonderfully unlikely
ways. Regard troubles as opportunities instead
of obstacles. As you rely on God, His glory will
shine through you—and
unexpected joy will be
your reward.

Justice

Benevolent Balance

What does the LORD require of you?
To act justly and to love mercy and
to walk humbly with your God.

MICAH 6:8 NIV

God is both merciful and just. His justice
demands that restitution be made for the
wrongs we've done. His mercy allows those
wrongs to be paid for in full when we put our
faith in Jesus' death and resurrection. One way
of thanking God for this benevolent balance is
by treating others fairly, mercifully, and with
humility. When we "do the right thing," we
love others the "right" way—a way that
reflects our heavenly Father's own
character.

Always Right and Just

Be ready! Let the truth be like a belt around your waist, and let God's justice protect you like armor.

EPHESIANS 6:14 CEV

A Roman soldier's belt was more than a fashion accessory. It held all of his offensive weapons. A soldier's defensive gear included a helmet, breastplate, and shield—his armor. As a woman of faith, God is your armor. When you're under attack, God not only offers you protection, He promises you justice. Secure your life with God's truth. Then rest in the fact that He's working behind the scenes, always doing what is right and just.

Kindness

Quiet Compassion

You've had a taste of God. Now, like infants at the breast, drink deep of God's pure kindness. Then you'll grow up mature and whole in God.

1 PETER 2:2-3 MSG

Kindness is the quiet compassion that flows from a loving heart. It doesn't announce its actions with shouts of "Look at me! Look what I did!" It whispers ever so gently, "Look at you. You're so worthy of love. Caring for you is my pleasure, my delight." Being the focus of an almighty King's kindness can be incredibly humbling, as well as encouraging. Let both humility and joy foster gratitude—and growth—in you.

Words and Actions

Everything depends on having faith in God, so that God's promise is assured by his great kindness.

ROMANS 4:16 CEV

A wise mother schools her children in the ways of kindness not only with her words but through her actions. God works the same way. Through the words of the Bible, God encourages His children to treat each other with respect, generosity, and consideration. But it's God's personal kindnesses to you that encourage your faith. Today, consider the many ways God has been kind to you just this week. What will your response be?

Leadership

Privilege

*If God has given you leadership ability,
take the responsibility seriously.*

ROMANS 12:8 NLT

It's a myth that lemmings will follow each
other off a cliff. The same can't be said
for people. Some people do unthinkable
things as the result of following a leader who
isn't worthy of admiration or imitation. If
God places you in a position of leadership,
whether at home, at work, at church, or in the
community, recognize it for the privilege it
is. Ask God to help you love those you
lead, guiding them with humility
and wisdom.

A Godly Leader

Good leadership is a channel of water controlled by God; he directs it to whatever ends he chooses.

PROVERBS 21:1 MSG

A good leader is a godly leader. She recognizes her strengths and uses them in a way that honors God and others. Most importantly, she recognizes her greatest asset is prayer. If you ask God for wisdom, He promises He'll give it to you. Whether you're leading executives in the boardroom or preschoolers through a lesson in sharing, ask God for the right words, right timing, and right attitude so you can wisely lead others in the right direction.

Learning

Pray Daily

Start with GOD—the first step in learning is bowing down to GOD.

PROVERBS 1:7 MSG

Before you could read, letters were meaningless squiggles on the page. But with practice and a parent's or teacher's help, one day everything clicked. Squiggles transformed into words—and words into stories. God is like those letters. However, you can't master the art of living by faith simply by studying about God. You need to humbly admit your wrongs. Accept God's forgiveness. Pray daily for growth and guidance. Then you'll learn who God really is and understand your part in His story.

Empowered by Prayer

Everything in the Scriptures is God's Word. All of it is useful for teaching and helping people and for correcting them and showing them how to live.

2 TIMOTHY 3:16 CEV

Your brain is an amazing, God-given gift. It enables you to master new skills, solve complex problems, and mature in your understanding of life. In short, it enables you to learn. By reading the Bible, you learn how to grow in your faith. As you read, ask yourself, "What does this teach me about loving God and/or others?" Then apply what you learn to your daily life. Your brain, empowered by prayer, will teach you how.

Life

Incredible Potential

*As obedient children, let yourselves
be pulled into a way of life shaped by
God's life, a life energetic and blazing
with holiness.*

1 PETER 1:15 MSG

Your life has incredible potential. It's filled
with opportunities to love, laugh, learn, and
make a positive difference in this world. Faith
turns every opportunity into an invitation:
Will you choose to live this moment in a way
that honors God? What you do with your life
matters. But ultimately, who you become
is more important than what you
accomplish. As your faith grows,
your heart more resembles God's
own. That's when you recognize
where your true potential lies.

Part of Life

Jesus said to her, "I am the resurrection
and the life. He who believes in Me,
though he may die, he shall live."

JOHN 11:25 NKJV

Death is a part of life, at least on this earth.
But because of Jesus, death is not something
to be feared. It's a door leading from this
life into the next. Faith is the key that opens
that door. Whenever this life leaves you
questioning, hurting, or longing for heaven,
picture yourself fingering that key. The more
tightly you hold on to your faith, the more
peace, hope, and joy you'll experience on this
side of that door.

Loneliness

Make the First Move

God sets the lonely in families.

PSALM 68:6 NIV

In the beginning of the Bible, God says it isn't good for people to be alone. Then He introduces Adam to Eve. The rest is history. Family is God's idea—and it's a good one. Whether it's your own family, your brothers and sisters in faith, or a time-tested circle of familial friends, don't wait for others to reach out to you when you're feeling lonely. Make the first move. True love both gives and receives.

Never Alone

*Jesus often withdrew to lonely places
and prayed.*

LUKE 5:16 NIV

Loneliness can make you feel like you're
on a deserted island surrounded by a sea of
people—yet no one notices you're there. But
there is someone who notices. Someone who'll
never leave you. Someone who won't forget
you or ignore you, no matter what you've done.
You may be lonely, but you're never alone.
Find a place of solace in the silence through
prayer. Loneliness may be the perfect lifeline
to draw you closer to God, the One whose love
will never fail.

Love

Essence of Love.

God is love.

1 JOHN 4:8 NIV

Burt Bacharach said it's what the world needs now. The Beatles told us it's all we need. Robert Palmer claimed it was addictive. Huey Lewis and the News talked about its power. What does God say about love? He says He's *it*, the essence of love itself. If, like the group Foreigner, you want to know what love is, look at Jesus. Everything He did, including sacrificing His own life, is what true love is all about.

Let Love Shine

What if I had faith that moved mountains? I would be nothing, unless I loved others.

1 CORINTHIANS 13:2 CEV

What mountain are you facing today? Perhaps it's the reconciliation of a relationship. Or maybe it's just that pile of laundry you've neglected. Whatever it is, it would be nice to simply "pray it away." But faith isn't a gift God gives to make life easier. Faith is God's classroom in which we learn how to become more loving—more like God Himself. Ask God to let love shine through in everything you do. Even sorting kids' socks.

Marriage

Focus

A wife of noble character who can find?
She is worth far more than rubies.

PROVERBS 31:10 NIV

Some wives are more precious than royal jewels. Others are royal pains. How does your husband see you? As you grow in your faith, you may notice how everyone around you could use the lessons you're learning. But God asks you to be responsible only for your own growth. Focus on loving your spouse by praying for him, helping him, and encouraging him. Be the spouse you'd like to be married to and let God handle the rest.

A Three-Legged Race

Marriage is not a place to "stand up for your rights." Marriage is a decision to serve the other.

1 CORINTHIANS 7:4 MSG

Marriage is like a three-legged race. Unless you work together, you're likely to take a few tumbles before crossing the finish line. Think of faith as the rope that holds you close. It binds you together, whether you're currently in sync or not. As you communicate with God and each other, God will help set your pace and direct your course. The more you allow God to humble your pride, the easier your relational race will be.

Nature

Aware of the Details

*By faith we understand that the
universe was formed at God's command,
so that what is seen was not made
out of what was visible.*

HEBREWS 11:3 NIV

It takes faith and science to appreciate the
wonders of nature. Science describes the
improbability of generations of butterflies
migrating thousands of miles to specific
destinations they've never experienced
firsthand or the impossibly delicate balance
of our orbiting solar system. Faith assures us
God not only understands miracles like these
but set them in motion. Surely, a
God who cares for the tiniest detail
of nature is aware—and at work—
in every detail of your life.

A Written Invitation

Ever since the world was created, people have seen the earth and sky. Through everything God made, they can clearly see his invisible qualities—his eternal power and divine nature.

ROMANS 1:20 NLT

God's story is written in more places than the Bible. It's written in the glory of the setting sun, the faithfulness of the ocean tides, the symphony of a thunderstorm, and the detail of a dragonfly's wing. It's written in every cell of you. Take time to "read" more about who God is as described through His creation. Contemplate His organizational skills, creative genius, and love of diversity. Consider nature God's written invitation to worship and wonder.

Patience

Half-Baked?

Let patience have its perfect work,
that you may be perfect
and complete, lacking nothing.

JAMES 1:4 NKJV

There's nothing delicious, delightful, or desirable about a half-baked cake. You have to wait until it's finished baking, no matter how hungry you are or how tight your time constraints may be. Impatience pushes us to take shortcuts and settle for second best. It can also rob us of opportunities to grow in our faith. The next time you feel impatience rising up in you, ask God, "What would You like me to learn while I wait?"

Always Hope

*Remember, the Lord's patience gives
people time to be saved.*
2 PETER 3:15 NLT

We're thankful for God's patience with us. He consistently honors us with time to grow, room to fail, and an endless supply of mercy and love. But we aren't the only ones who benefit from His patience. He extends it to everyone, including those we feel are slow learners or those we consider hopeless cases. In God's eyes and in God's timing, there's always hope. Ask God to help you extend to others what He so graciously extends to you.

Peace

Permanent Peace

Since we have been made right in God's sight by faith, we have peace with God because of what Jesus Christ our Lord has done for us.

ROMANS 5:1 NLT

When world leaders sign a peace treaty, they pledge to keep the terms of an agreement. They aren't agreeing to like it—or each other. When you put your faith in Christ's sacrifice on your behalf, you make peace with God. God pledges to forgive your past grievances and even future mistakes. But the peace between you and God is more than an agreement. It's the rebirth of a relationship. This peace is permanent, based on unconditional love, not legality.

A Perfect Complement

*"I am leaving you with a gift—peace
of mind and heart. And the peace
I give is a gift the world cannot give.
So don't be troubled or afraid."*

JOHN 14:27 NLT

When attending a going-away party, it's customary to give a gift to the one who's going away. Jesus turned this concept on its head, as He so often did with the status quo. At the Last Supper, the day before He died, Jesus gave all of His followers a gift—peace. When you choose to follow Jesus, you receive this gift. You'll find it fits your life perfectly, complementing any and every circumstance.

Perseverance

A Fresh Start

*I have fought the good fight, I have
finished the race, I have kept the faith.*

2 TIMOTHY 4:7 NKJV

Faith is more like a marathon than a leisurely
jog through the park. During some legs of the
race, you'll be feeling strong and confident.
During others, you may find yourself
stumbling over questions, losing sight of the
right path, or wanting to sit on the sidelines.
To keep moving forward, run the race of faith
one step at a time. Consider each day a fresh
starting line. Moment by moment, with God's
help, you will persevere.

Lean on Him

Consider him who endured such opposition from sinners, so that you will not grow weary and lose heart.

HEBREWS 12:3 NIV

Jesus literally went through hell for you. He suffered the pain of rejection and betrayal. He endured physical agony. He gave His life out of love for you. When you face what seems unendurable, hold on to Jesus. Cry out to Him for help and hope. Pray throughout the day, picturing Him by your side, holding you up when your own strength fails. Express your love for Him by leaning on Him. He's near to help you persevere.

Power

"Yes!"

We pray for God's power to help you do all the good things that you hope to do and that your faith makes you want to do.

2 Thessalonians 1:11 CEV

Faith gives you the desire—and power—to do things you may have never even dreamed of attempting before. Serving meals to the homeless. Leading a Bible study. Praying for an ailing coworker. Sharing your personal story aloud in church. Forgiving someone who's betrayed you. The more you grow in your faith, the more God will stretch your idea of who you are—and what you can do. Through God's power, you can confidently say *yes!* to doing anything He asks.

Power Source

We are like clay jars in which this treasure is stored. The real power comes from God and not from us.

2 CORINTHIANS 4:7 CEV

What happens if your blow dryer won't blow? First, you check out the power source. Without power, a blow dryer may look useful, but it's really nothing more than a plastic knickknack. Likewise, it's God's power working through you that allows you to accomplish more than you can on your own. Staying connected with God through prayer, obedience, reading the Bible, and loving others well will keep His power flowing freely into your life—and out into the world.

Praise

Out of Love

If you are having trouble, you should pray. And if you are feeling good, you should sing praises.

JAMES 5:13 CEV

If you're a mom, you know your children will ask for help more frequently than they'll express their thanks. You also know that much of what you do behind the scenes will never receive a word of praise. Of course, that's not why you do it. You do what you do out of love. The same is true of God. Why not take some time today to praise your heavenly Father for all the little ways He shows His love.

Because of You

When your faith remains strong through many trials, it will bring you much praise and glory and honor on the day when Jesus Christ is revealed to the whole world.

1 PETER 1:7 NLT

The thought of God praising you may be a new one. But when Jesus returns, what you've done and overcome because of your faith will be visible to all. But it's not the accolades of others that make this worth anticipating. It's the chance to see God smile—and know it's because of you. In this life, you may feel your efforts go unnoticed. Rejoice in knowing God sees and praises everything you do because of your faith in Him.

Prayer

Easy to Recognize

*Be joyful in hope, patient in affliction,
faithful in prayer.*

ROMANS 12:12 NIV

How do you build a relationship with a friend? You spend time together. You talk about everything, openly sharing your hearts. Prayer is simply talking to your best Friend. True, it's harder to understand God's reply than it is to read a friend's text or pick up her phone message. But the more frequently you pray, the easier it is to recognize God's voice.

So keep talking. God's listening. With time, you'll learn how to listen in return.

In Line with the Truth

*Everything you ask for in prayer will be
yours, if you only have faith.*

MARK 11:24 CEV

Faith keeps our prayers in line with the truth
behind what we say we believe. If we believe
God loves us, believe Jesus is who He said
He was, believe God has a plan for our lives,
believe He's good, wise, and just—our prayers
will reflect these beliefs. They'll be in line
with God's will—with what God desires for our
life. These are the kind of prayers God assures
us He'll answer, in His time and His way.

Presence of God

Draw Near

I walk in the LORD's presence as I live here on earth!

PSALM 116:9 NLT

At times, God's presence is elusive. Although you believe in Him, you forget He's there. But He's like the air around you: invisible, yet essential to life. Remind yourself of God's presence each morning as soon as you awake. Breathe in and thank God for His gift of life. Then breathe out, asking Him to make you more aware of His hand at work in your life. Throughout the day, just breathe—drawing near to the One who gave you breath.

Always Welcome

*Because of Christ and our faith in him,
we can now come boldly and
confidently into God's presence.*

EPHESIANS 3:12 NLT

Being in the presence of someone you've
wronged isn't a comfortable place to be.
Even after apologies have been offered and
restitution made, a feeling of shame and
unworthiness often lingers. This isn't the case
in our relationship with God. When we set
things straight through faith, all that lingers is
God's love. Draw close to God in prayer. Never
be afraid to enter His presence. You're always
welcome, just as you are.

Priorities

God First

"Seek the Kingdom of God above all else, and live righteously, and he will give you everything you need."

MATTHEW 6:33 NLT

Putting God first sounds like the right thing to do. But what does that look like in real life? Does it mean spending every moment reading the Bible or praying over questions like, "Paper or plastic?" Holding God's Kingdom as your top priority simply means that God's way becomes your way. Each day, ask God to help you live and love in a way that makes Him proud. Then watch Him provide what you need to do what He asks.

God's Priority for You

Honor Christ and put others first.

EPHESIANS 5:21 CEV

Eating, sleeping, working, praying, paying bills, staying fit, spending time with those you love. . .there are so many different priorities that cry out for your time each day. If you're struggling to figure out how to balance them all, allow your faith to help put things in perspective. What's God's priority for you? That you live a life of love and integrity. Keep these two things in mind as you decide what to add and remove from your schedule today.

Protection

Saved and Secure

You have faith in God, whose power will protect you until the last day. Then he will save you, just as he has always planned to do.

1 PETER 1:5 CEV

Life can seem pretty precarious. The evening news fills our heads and hearts with stories of disaster and demise. In light of it all, our bodies appear so fragile. But the Bible tells us God has numbered our days. He's planned the day of our birth and the day we'll die. Nothing and no one can alter those plans. Like your future, your faith is under God's sovereign care. Within the power of His protection, you're saved and secure.

Shelter from the Storm

God's a safe-house for the battered,
a sanctuary during bad times.
The moment you arrive, you relax; you're
never sorry you knocked.

PSALM 9:9-10 MSG

Your pumps are caked in mud. Your hair clings like a damp rag, and you smell a bit like a wet schnauzer. But the rain doesn't let up. All you want is a warm, dry spot—a shelter from the storm. The Bible says you'll face all kinds of storms in this life. But God's your safe place, regardless of what's raging all around you. He's with you in every storm, offering protection and peace. Don't hesitate to draw near.

Provision

Far Beyond the Basics

God will generously provide all you need. Then you will always have everything you need and plenty left over to share with others.

2 CORINTHIANS 9:8 NLT

*N*eed is an easy word to use—and abuse. "I need new shoes to go with this outfit." "I need chocolate, right here, right now!" "I need some respect!" When God says He'll provide what we need, it's always on His terms, not ours. He provides everything we need to do everything He's asked us to do. Yet our loving God goes far beyond supplying the basics. He surprises us by filling to overflowing needs we never even knew we had.

Wholeness

Jesus declared, "I am the bread of life.
Whoever comes to me will never go
hungry, and whoever believes in me
will never be thirsty."

JOHN 6:35 NIV

When we talk about provision, our physical
needs first come to mind: food, water, shelter,
and the like. But we have spiritual needs that
are just as essential as the air we breathe. We
thirst for God's forgiveness and hunger for
His love. Those who haven't yet put their faith
in God often try filling this need with power,
possessions, or relationships. But only a
relationship with God can fill this void. Only
faith provides wholeness to a broken world.

Purpose

True Purpose

Now the purpose of the commandment is love from a pure heart, from a good conscience, and from sincere faith.

1 TIMOTHY 1:5 NKJV

Did you do that on purpose?" Any mom who asks a child this question should be ready to carefully weigh the answer. But how about you? Consider what you've done this week. How much of it was truly "on purpose"? Faith provides a singular purpose for living: to love God and others. Fulfilling this purpose requires living prayerfully and with intention. Today, ask God to help slow you down. Consider your true purpose as you make your plans.

Set in Stone

We humans keep brainstorming options and plans, but GOD's purpose prevails.

PROVERBS 19:21 MSG

When people mention "the best-laid plans," they're usually bemoaning how the unexpected derailed what once seemed like a sure thing. God's the Master of the unexpected. That doesn't mean planning is a bad thing. It helps us use time, money, and resources in a more efficient way. But the only plans that are set in stone are God's own. Make sure your plans are in line with God's purposes. That's the wisest thing you can do to assure success.

Relationships

Beyond Your Comfort Zone

God wants us to have faith in his Son Jesus Christ and to love each other. This is also what Jesus taught us to do.

1 JOHN 3:23 CEV

People matter to God. All kinds of people. From celebrities to "nobodies," pompous people to selfless servants, atheists to those martyred for their faith. If people matter to God, they should also matter to you. It's easy to invest yourself only in relationships that feel comfortable and personally beneficial. But faith sees beyond social circles and stereotypes. Ask God to help you reach beyond your relational comfort zone. You may be surprised by the gift of a friend for life.

Toward Unconditional Love

*You can develop a healthy, robust
community that lives right with God and
enjoy its results only if you do the hard
work of getting along with each other.*

JAMES 3:18 MSG

What are your greatest accomplishments?
Earning a degree? Landing a big account?
Lovingly leading a toddler through the terrible
twos? Whatever you've accomplished, hard
work undoubtedly played a part in your
success. The same goes for relationships.
Going beyond superficiality toward
unconditional love is hard work. It's a
relational journey that takes patience,
perseverance, forgiveness, humility, and
sacrifice. It's a journey God willingly took to
build a relationship with you. Now it's your
turn to follow in His relational footsteps.

Renewal

Restart

*You're my place of quiet retreat; I wait
for your Word to renew me.*

PSALM 119:114 MSG

If your computer has a glitch, it's helpful
to refresh the page or reboot the whole
program by pushing RESTART. God helps us
refresh, reboot, and restart by renewing us
through His Spirit. When you're in need of
refreshment—even if you've already spent
time with God that day reading the Bible,
singing His praises, or praying—take time to
sit quietly in God's presence. Push RESTART.
Wait patiently and expectantly for a word from
the One you love.

God Supplies

Those who hope in the LORD will renew their strength. They will soar on wings like eagles; they will run and not grow weary.

ISAIAH 40:31 NIV

Every woman has days when she's feeling weary. But sometimes, this feels more like the norm than just a down day. When this happens, welcome weariness as a messenger. It's a reminder you're in need of renewal. Get alone with God and ask, "Is there anything I need to change? What's out of my hands and in Yours alone?" Allow God to do His job. Then through the strength God supplies, do what you can with what you have.

Respect

Your Heart

A kindhearted woman gains [respect].
PROVERBS 11:16 NIV

Aretha Franklin sang about the importance of getting a little "R-E-S-P-E-C-T." But what's worthy of respect in God's eyes? In the corporate world, power and prestige usually herald respect. But God doesn't care about your title or notoriety. He cares about your heart, about how you treat others. Treating all of those God loves with kindness is one way of respecting both them and God—and receiving a little "R-E-S-P-E-C-T" in return.

Ultimate Authority Figure

Everything you were taught can be put into a few words: Respect and obey God! This is what life is all about.

ECCLESIASTES **12:13** CEV

As a little girl, chances are you were taught to respect authority. Parents, teachers, police officers, the elderly—people whose relationship, experience, or profession put them in a position of influence over your life were deemed worthy of honor and obedience. Now, as a woman of faith, you've accepted God as the ultimate authority figure over you. Don't let that title scare you. God's love tempers the power of His position. Respecting Him is just one more way of worshipping Him.

Rest

His Company

"Are you tired? Worn out? Burned out on religion? Come to me. Get away with me and you'll recover your life. I'll show you how to take a real rest."

MATTHEW 11:28-29 MSG

Faith is not a to-do list of assignments from God. It's an invitation to relationship. It's about getting to know who God is and who He created you to be. It's about resting in God's love and acceptance, not working harder to prove yourself worthy of His affection. If you're suffering from spiritual burnout, take time to simply relax in God's presence, enjoying His company the way He enjoys yours.

Time to Rest

*It is useless for you to work so hard
from early morning until late at night,
anxiously working for food to eat; for
God gives rest to his loved ones.*

PSALM 127:2 NLT

For three years, Jesus devoted His life to spreading the good news about God's love. This was an incredibly important job, one with eternal consequences. But even Jesus took time to rest. Although He dined with friends, taught, preached, and performed miracles, many times He left spiritually hungry crowds behind to spend time alone with His heavenly Father. You have many important roles to fill in this life. Rest is one of God's gifts that can empower you to accomplish what He's given you to do.

Reward

Desired Reward

It is impossible to please God without faith. Anyone who wants to come to him must believe that God exists and that he rewards those who sincerely seek him.

HEBREWS 11:6 NLT

Ultimately, it's not what you do but what you believe that's rewarded by God. You can fill your life with good deeds, even to the point of sacrificing your life. But if your faith is in your own strength, abilities, or goodness—instead of God—your full reward will be the praise of those around you. However, if you're motivated by faith, the only reward you'll desire is pleasing God. Having faith in God truly is its own reward.

Gold Crowns

*"The LORD rewards people who
are faithful and live right."*

1 SAMUEL 26:23 CEV

Exactly how God rewards His children is a bit
of a mystery. The Bible tells us we'll receive
gold crowns in heaven, which we'll promptly
cast at Jesus' feet to honor Him. But the Bible
also talks about rewards in this life. Our
rewards may be delivered in tangible ways,
such as through success or financial gain.
But our reward may also be a more intangible
treasure, such as contentment and joy.
Treasures like these will never tarnish or
grow old.

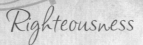

Righteousness

Wiped Away

God, with undeserved kindness, declares that we are righteous. He did this through Christ Jesus when he freed us from the penalty for our sins.

ROMANS 3:24 NLT

Saying you're righteous is the same as saying you're blameless. And that's what God says about you. Once you put your faith and trust in Jesus, every trace of your past rebellion against God is wiped away. It's as though you lived Jesus' life, morally perfect and wholly good. What's more, this righteousness covers your future as well as your past. Anytime you stumble, go straight to God. Confess what you've done. You can trust it's forgiven *and* forgotten.

The Loving Choice

Pursue a righteous life—a life of wonder, faith, love, steadiness, courtesy. Run hard and fast in the faith.

1 TIMOTHY 6:11-12 MSG

Wearing white after Labor Day used to be considered taboo. But what was accepted as "right" in your mother's generation is not always considered "right" today. With God, the rules never change. What's right is always right. Living a righteous life means consistently choosing to do what's right in God's eyes. Doing what's right may not always be the popular choice, but it will always be the loving choice, the one God would make if He were in your shoes.

Sacrifice

God's Favorite Gift

*"Obedience is better than sacrifice,
and submission is better than
offering the fat of rams."*

1 SAMUEL 15:22 NLT

Suppose you had a daughter who broke every rule you made. She jumped on the furniture, hit her little brother, and swiped money from your wallet. Every day. But every evening, she offered you her dessert, telling you how much she loved you. The next day it was disobedience as usual. Have you ever been that little girl in God's eyes? Making sacrifices in God's name is commendable. But first, do what God asks. Obedience is God's favorite gift.

Glorious Benefits

God sent Christ to be our sacrifice. Christ offered his life's blood, so that by faith in him we could come to God.

ROMANS 3:25 CEV

It's easy to focus solely on the glorious benefits of believing in God. Gifts like forgiveness, eternal life, a fresh start, and unconditional love are certainly worth celebrating. But each of these gifts comes at a very high cost. Jesus paid for them with His life. Jesus' sacrifice involved physical suffering, humiliation, betrayal, and separation from His Father. Choosing to follow Jesus will involve sacrifice on your part. Allow Him to show you how sacrifice can lead to something good.

Salvation

Found

Salvation is not a reward for the good things we have done, so none of us can boast about it.

EPHESIANS 2:9 NLT

You're lost at sea, drowning. There's no hope of saving yourself. Then members of the Coast Guard appear. They pull you from the frigid water—no questions asked. They don't save you because of your impressive resume or because you're such a kind woman. They save you because you need saving. Jesus saved you because you took hold of His hand in faith when He offered to pull you from the waves. Without Him, you were lost. Now, you're found—saved and secure.

Nothing More. . .or Less!

*"Jesus is the one. . . .
There is salvation in no one else!
God has given no other name under
heaven by which we must be saved."*

ACTS 4:11-12 NLT

God created you to live forever with Him.
But like every other person since the dawn of
time, you turned away from God to live life
on your own terms. Yet God didn't give up on
you. He sent His Son to pay the heavy price of
your rebellion, to sacrifice His life for yours.
When you place your faith in Jesus, you accept
this gift. Your salvation's complete. There's
nothing more—or less—that you can do to be
saved.

Security

Secure and Immovable

I am sure that nothing can separate us from God's love—not life or death, not angels or spirits, not the present or the future.

ROMANS 8:38 CEV

You can feel secure in your relationship with God. God doesn't suffer from mood swings or bad hair days. He isn't swayed by popular opinion or influenced by what others have to say about you. God's love, His character, His gift of salvation, and every promise He's ever made to you stands firm, immovable. You can lean on Him in any and every circumstance, secure in the fact that He'll never let you down.

The Ultimate Bodyguard

*Fear of the L*ORD *leads to life, bringing
security and protection from harm.*

PROVERBS **19:23** NLT

Fear sounds like a rather dubious route to
take to find security. After all, you wouldn't
hire a personal bodyguard whom you feared
would harm you. But fearing God isn't the
same as being afraid of Him. Fearing God
means standing in awe of Him. After all,
He's the almighty Creator, our sovereign
Master, the righteous Judge of all. But this
all-powerful God is *for* you. He's on your
side, fighting on your behalf. Talk about the
ultimate bodyguard!

Self-control

Attractive

*Better to be patient than powerful;
better to have self-control
than to conquer a city.*

PROVERBS 16:32 NLT

Self-control is attractive, to others and to
God. That's because self-control reflects
God's own character. God doesn't act out
a whim. He waits for just the right time to
do just the right thing. Is there any area of
your life where you wish you had more self-
control? God can help. Perhaps you need to
lose weight, just say no to gossip, or keep your
temper in check. Ask God for the desire and
the discipline to wisely exercise restraint.

Under Control

*The Spirit God gave us does not make
us timid, but gives us power,
love and self-discipline.*

2 TIMOTHY 1:7 NIV

Have you ever excused your own poor behavior by saying, "That's just the way I am"? God's Spirit tells a different story about who you are. Through faith, you have the ability to live a life characterized by discipline and self-control. But the choice to live that life is up to you. Consider the "character flaws" you see in yourself. Ask God to help you get these areas under control, one thought, word, or action at a time.

175

Serving God

The Big Picture

See how Abraham's faith and deeds worked together. He proved that his faith was real by what he did.

JAMES 2:22 CEV

Abraham wholeheartedly believed in God's power and love. So when God told Abraham to sacrifice his long-awaited son, Abraham prepared to do exactly what God asked. Surely Abraham had questions. He didn't know how everything would turn out. In the end, God saved Isaac and commended Abraham's faith. Serving God isn't always an easy path. You may not see the big picture behind what you're asked to do. But you can trust God's plan for you is good.

Faith into Action

Offer your bodies to him as a living sacrifice, pure and pleasing. That's the most sensible way to serve God.

ROMANS 12:1 CEV

The most important choice you'll ever make is whether to serve God or yourself. The good news is that by choosing to serve God, you wind up doing what's best for yourself, as well. Caring for the body God's given you is one way of serving Him. That includes eating a healthy diet, exercising regularly, getting annual checkups, and using your body in ways that honor God and others. It's just one more way of putting your faith into action.

Singleness

The "Single" Gift

I wish everyone were single, just as I am. But God gives to some the gift of marriage, and to others the gift of singleness.

1 CORINTHIANS 7:7 NLT

Do you consider singleness a gift? Paul did. He was one of the most prolific writers in the New Testament. His letters to churches like the one in Corinth teach us a lot about what living a life of faith looks like. He believed that being single gave him more time and freedom to focus more fully on God. Ask God to reveal to you how being single at this time is a gift for you.

Walk with Him

The LORD All-Powerful, the Holy
God of Israel, rules all the earth.
He is your Creator and husband,
and he will rescue you.

ISAIAH **54:5** CEV

Being single by choice feels different than
being single by circumstance. If you deeply
desire to be married or if your spouse has
passed away, you may struggle with feelings of
loneliness, discontent, and even resentment
toward God. If these feelings arise, don't
bury yourself in them. Take them straight
to God. Honestly tell Him how you feel. God
loves you like a father, friend, lover, husband,
and deliverer. Walk with Him. He'll lead you
toward healing and wholeness.

Sleep

A Favorite Lullaby

*I think about you before I go to sleep,
and my thoughts turn to you
during the night.*

PSALM 63:6 CEV

Sleep can be elusive, particularly during certain seasons of a woman's life. If 2:00 a.m. feedings, the throes of menopause, or simply mentally sorting through the demands of daily life are keeping you awake, set aside your frustration. Picture yourself pulling up the blanket of darkness, settling into the silence of night. Then turn your thoughts to God.

Pour out your problems or lift up your praises. Ask God for refreshment and renewal. Allow God's voice to become your favorite lullaby.

Sound Sleep

*The LORD is your protector, and he
won't go to sleep or let you stumble.*

PSALM 121:3 CEV

For small children, bedtime can be a scary
time. They may be afraid of the dark, of
monsters lurking under their bed, or of bad
dreams disturbing their slumber. Bedtime
prayers can help calm their fears. They can
calm yours, as well. Knowing God never
sleeps can help you sleep more soundly. If
you're in the dark about a certain situation, if
"monsters" are threatening your peace, take
your concerns to God. It's never too late to
call out to Him.

Speech

A Story to Tell

It is with your heart that you believe and are justified, and it is with your mouth that you profess your faith and are saved.

ROMANS 10:10 NIV

For some people, faith is a very private part of their lives. But you have a story to tell that others need to hear. Sharing how God is at work in your life gives others permission to ask spiritual questions. Don't worry about not having all the answers. You can't. An infinite God will always be bigger than our finite minds can comprehend. But saying aloud what you believe is part of living and growing in your faith.

The Power of Words

Let everything you say be good and helpful, so that your words will be an encouragement to those who hear them.

EPHESIANS 4:29 NLT

Research tells us that women speak about twice as many words as men do each day. That gives us twice as many reasons to pay attention to what we say! It's easy to let whatever pops into our heads pop out of our mouths, but the Bible reminds us that our words have power. We're responsible for how we use that power. Will we hurt or heal? Build up or tear down? Allow faith to help you choose wisely.

Spiritual Growth

Blossoms

The godly will flourish like palm trees. . . . Even in old age they will still produce fruit; they will remain vital and green.

PSALM 92:12, 14 NLT

As you grow close to God, you blossom spiritually. But this is one flower that will never fade or fall. Your body will age, but spiritually you'll continue to grow stronger and more beautiful. The more time you spend with God, the more your character will begin to resemble His—and the more humble you'll find yourself in His presence. This is exactly the kind of woman God's looking for to do wonderful things in this world.

Beautiful Things

Do your best to improve your faith.
You can do this by adding goodness,
understanding, self-control, patience,
devotion to God, concern for
others, and love.

2 PETER 1:5-7 CEV

Only God can make a seed grow. But you can
make conditions favorable to help that seed
mature and bear fruit. The same is true with
faith. Cultivate through obedience the seed
of faith God has planted in you. When God
reveals a weed budding in your character,
pull it up by the roots. A fresh sprout of love?
Water it regularly with kindness and sacrifice.
Tend to your spiritual growth each day, and
beautiful things will begin to take root.

Strength

Step-by-Step

I can do everything through Christ,
who gives me strength.

PHILIPPIANS 4:13 NLT

Picture yourself in a race, struggling to reach the finish line. You're exhausted, discouraged, perhaps even injured. You're tempted to give up. Then a friend runs onto the course from the sidelines. She places her arm around your waist, inviting you to lean on her for strength and support. Together, step-by-step, you see the race to completion. God is that kind of Friend. Whether the strength you need today is physical, emotional, or spiritual, God is there. Lean on Him.

A Second Wind

Strength is for service, not status. Each one of us needs to look after the good of the people around us, asking ourselves, "How can I help?"

ROMANS 15:1 MSG

When you're feeling worn out, it's hard to think about meeting anyone's needs other than your own. But sometimes that's exactly what God asks you to do. Perhaps it's your children who need your help in the middle of the night. Or maybe it's a stranger whose car has broken down by the side of the road. When God nudges you to respond, call on Him for strength. His Spirit will rouse your compassion, providing you with a second wind.

Success

In Line with God's Goals

*Commit to the LORD whatever you do,
and he will establish your plans.*

PROVERBS 16:3 NIV

Faith's definition of *success* differs from that of the world. Whereas our culture applauds people of fame, wealth, and power, faith regards those who live their lives according to God's purpose as successful. Committing whatever you do to God isn't asking Him to bless what you've already decided to do. It's inviting Him into the planning process. Make sure your dreams and goals are in line with God's. Then get to work— leaving the end result in His hands.

Consistent Effort

"The market is flooded with surefire, easygoing formulas for a successful life. . . . The way to life—to God!—is vigorous and requires total attention."

MATTHEW 7:13-14 MSG

Some people confuse luck with success. They want the reward of a successful life without having to put in the work. But success is something that's achieved over time. Whether it's in the workplace, parenting your children, or growing in your faith, success is the result of consistent effort toward reaching a goal. A successful life is made up of successful days—and a truly successful day is one that draws you closer to God and His plans for you.

Thankfulness

God at Work

Give thanks in all circumstances; for this is God's will for you in Christ Jesus.

1 THESSALONIANS 5:18 NIV

Faith gives you new eyes, along with a new heart. As you look more consistently in God's direction, you become aware of things you never noticed before. . .the miraculous detail of God's creation, the countless gifts He gives each day, His answers to prayer, and His persistence in bringing something positive out of even the most negative circumstances. It's good to notice God at work. It's even better to say "thank you" when you do. What will you thank Him for today?

Special People

I have not stopped giving thanks for you, remembering you in my prayers.

EPHESIANS 1:16 NIV

There are many ways of showing gratitude. You can send flowers or share a hug. You can say "thanks" with a note, text, e-mail, or phone call. But have you ever considered expressing your gratitude via prayer? Asking for God's guidance and blessing on those who've generously touched your life with their love takes thankfulness to the next level—an eternal one. It also reminds you to thank God for His gift of bringing these special people into your life.

Thoughts

Changed Minds

*Create pure thoughts in me and
make me faithful again.*

PSALM 51:10 CEV

Living a life that pleases God is more than
doing the right thing. It's also thinking the
right thing. That's because faith isn't about
appearances. It's about reality. It's about
all of you: body, mind, and spirit. This
transformation doesn't happen overnight. But
the more time you spend with God, the more
aware you'll become of random thoughts that
don't line up with your faith. Take
those thoughts to God. Ask Him to
help change your mind for good.

Flip the Switch

*Keep your minds on whatever is true,
pure, right, holy, friendly, and proper.
Don't ever stop thinking about what is
truly worthwhile and worthy of praise.*

PHILIPPIANS 4:8 CEV

Some trains of thought need to be derailed.
That's because they don't lead you closer to
becoming the woman God created you to be.
But like a switch operator who changes the
track a train is on to save it from disaster, you
can change the direction of your thoughts.
If others could read your mind and you'd
be embarrassed by what they read, flip the
switch. Choose to focus on something worthy
of your time and God's praise.

Trust

What Lies Ahead

The word of the LORD holds true, and we can trust everything he does.

PSALM 33:4 NLT

You confide in a friend because she's proven herself faithful over time. She won't lie. What she says she'll do, she does. You trust in her love because you believe she has your best interests at heart. God is this kind of friend. It takes time to build your own track record of trust with Him. As you do, consider His faithfulness to those in the Bible. God's past faithfulness can help you trust Him for whatever lies ahead.

The Little and Big Things

*Trust in the LORD with all your heart,
and lean not on your own
understanding.*

PROVERBS 3:5 NKJV

If you lean against a wall, you have faith in its integrity. You trust it won't crumble and leave you in a heap on the floor. If you trust God, you'll lean on Him. This is more than saying, "I believe." This is living what you believe. You may not always understand the "whys" behind God's ways, but the more you risk trusting Him with the little things, the more confident you'll be entrusting Him with the big ones.

Truth

Trust the Truth

Jesus answered, "I am the way and the truth and the life. No one comes to the Father except through me."

JOHN 14:6 NIV

Believing all good people go to heaven sounds nice. But it doesn't make sense. How do you measure goodness? Where's the cutoff between being "in" and being "out"? Spiritual truths cannot be relative or change according to how we feel. They must be timeless, steadfast—like Jesus. Jesus said that putting our faith in Him is the only way we can be reconciled with God and receive eternal life. Trust the truth. Trust Jesus.

Wholly True

*Lead blameless lives and do
what is right, speaking the truth
from sincere hearts.*

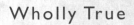

PSALM 15:2 NLT

The truth can't be twisted or stretched. It can't masquerade as a "half truth" or a "little white lie." If what you say isn't wholly true, it isn't the truth. Period. Speaking the truth doesn't mean saying aloud every thought that enters your head. It means passing out words like gifts. Choose each one carefully. Then wrap it in love and respect. Be as honest and truthful with others as God has been with you.

Waiting

The Perfect Harvest

The Lord longs to be gracious to you; therefore he will rise up to show you compassion. For the Lord is a God of justice. Blessed are all who wait for him!

ISAIAH 30:18 NIV

God is the Master of perfect timing because He can see straight across the grand scheme of history. He can tell if what you're waiting for today would be even better if it was received tomorrow—or years down the road. As you grow in your faith, you'll grow to trust God's timing more and more. Expect Him to surprise you with the perfect harvest always delivered at exactly the right time.

Keep Watching

I wait for the Lord more than watchmen wait for the morning.

PSALM 130:6 NIV

If asked about your favorite pastime, chances are "waiting" will never make it to the top of your list. But waiting is not wasted time. It's growing time. It's time to stay alert, to keep watch, to look for signs that God's on the move. You're like a watchman waiting for sunrise. You know it's coming. You see signs of its arrival before it's fully dawn. Whatever you're waiting on God for today, keep watching. He's on the way.

Wholeness

Put Together Perfectly

GOD made my life complete when I placed all the pieces before him.

PSALM 18:20 MSG

Your life is a bit like a jigsaw puzzle, made up of multiple pieces. Some pieces are things you do. Others are things you are, have been, or hope to become one day. Your physical body, your emotional makeup, and the unique way your brain works are all part of this puzzle. To fully trust in God, you need to place every piece in His hands. Only God has the power to put you together perfectly.

Healed and Whole

*God is keeping careful watch over us
and the future. The Day is coming when
you'll have it all—life healed and whole.*

1 PETER 1:5 MSG

When you reach out in faith, God starts the
process of healing old wounds. But there are
some wounds that won't completely heal this
side of heaven. Like a former injury that aches
with an approaching storm, past emotional
scars may ache at unexpected times. Scars
are signs of healing, a step toward wholeness.
Thank God for the healing He's brought your
way and know that when Jesus returns, He'll
wipe away every tear. That's when you'll truly
be healed and whole.

Wisdom

Incomparably Wise

*The fear of the LORD is
the beginning of wisdom.*

PSALM 111:10 NIV

Only God sees the big picture of your life in
the context of the past, present, and future. He
not only sees this picture, He has the power to
transform it. In addition, God is incomparably
wise, so He knows the best way this
transformation can be accomplished. Trusting
God with your life shows wisdom on your part.
The more closely you follow where He leads,
the more your own wisdom will grow.

Wisdom at Work

There's nothing better than being wise,
knowing how to interpret the
meaning of life. Wisdom puts
light in the eyes, and gives gentleness
to words and manners.

ECCLESIASTES 8:1 MSG

Wisdom not only knows the right thing
to do, it knows the right time and place to
do it. As you grow in your faith, you can't
help but grow in this kind of wisdom. That's
what happens when you spend time with an
all-wise God. His character rubs off on you.
As you more clearly see others from God's
perspective, you'll grow wiser in how you put
your God-inspired love into action. Put your
wisdom to work today.

Work

Your Best

Whatever you say or do should be done in the name of the Lord Jesus, as you give thanks to God the Father because of him.

COLOSSIANS 3:17 CEV

Your faith should affect your work in wonderfully positive ways. Whether you work outside the home or not, whether you love your job or are doing it simply to pay the bills, tackle every job as if you were doing it for God Himself. Be honest, diligent, and gracious. Give yourself wholeheartedly to the task at hand, no matter how small. Give God your best by doing your best. He gave His best for you.

Measured Efforts

Pay careful attention to your own work, for then you will get the satisfaction of a job well done, and you won't need to compare yourself to anyone else.

GALATIANS 6:4 NLT

Faith helps you focus on what's most important in life—and in work. But when you're working hard, it can be frustrating to be around people who are not. Instead of taking them to task, take them to God in prayer. Ask for wisdom in knowing what to do or say, or if you should take any action at all. Measure your own efforts against what God's asked you to do instead of the efforts of those around you.

Worship

Circle of Love

Worship GOD if you want the best;
worship opens doors to all his goodness.

PSALM 34:9 MSG

When you worship God, you look at Him. You focus on who He is and what He's done. The thanks, the prayers, the songs, and the actions that flow out of this time are all different forms of worshipping the One who's given you life—and so much more. When you focus on God, you see more clearly how closely He's focusing on you. Worship weaves a reciprocal circle of love, one that will never end.

A Fresh Invitation

God gave Christ the highest place and honored his name above all others. So at the name of Jesus everyone will bow down, those in heaven, on earth, and under the earth.

PHILIPPIANS 2:9-10 CEV

One day, everyone will know that what you believe is absolutely true. Jesus, the focus of your faith, will be visible to all. Every created being will fall facedown in awe at the mere mention of His name. But you don't have to wait until then. Each new day delivers a fresh invitation to worship, countless more reasons to lift up your praise. Worship is a song that has no end. What verse will your life sing to Jesus today?

Scripture Index

Old Testament

Proverbs

New Testament

Mark

Luke

John

Acts

1 Peter

2 Peter

1 John

Notes

Notes

Notes

Notes

Notes